# BURNED ALIVE

a true story

DAVID KENNETH POLETZ

Copyright © 2020 David Kenneth Poletz

ISBN:
978-1-952874-35-2 (paperback)
978-1-952874-36-9 (hardback)
978-1-952874-37-6 (ebook)

All rights reserved. No part of this publication may be reproduced, stored in a retrieval system, or transmitted in any form or by any means - electronic, mechanical, photocopy, recording, scanning, or other – except for brief quotations in critical reviews or articles, without the prior written permission of the publisher.

Printed in New York by:

OMNIBOOK CO.
99 Wall Street, Suite 118
New York, NY 10005
USA
+1-866-216-9965
www.omnibookcompany.com

For e-book purchase: Kindle on Amazon, Barnes and Noble
Book purchase: Amazon.com, Barnes & Noble, and
**www.omnibookcompany.com**

Omnibook titles may be purchased in bulk for educational, business, fund-raising, or sales promotional use. For more information please e-mail info@omnibookcompany.com

# CONTENTS

| | |
|---|---|
| Introduction | 1 |
| Chapter 1 | 3 |
| Chapter 2 | 11 |
| Chapter 3 | 15 |
| Chapter 4 | 23 |
| Chapter 5 | 27 |
| Chapter 6 | 33 |
| Chapter 7 | 39 |

# Introduction

I am writing this book to maybe prevent somebody else from going through the same terror I endured. The pain and suffering were just about unbearable. This is a true story about a very bad accident that happened in Lloydminster, Alberta, on March 25, 1992. I survived it, but I have many scars and losses. Doctors gave me a very small (5 percent) chance of living through this accident. My left leg was amputated below the knee, all my fingers were amputated on my left hand, and I also had burns covering 44 percent of my body. I had a tracheotomy to improve my breathing at the time. I sustained a very mild brain injury due to the lack of oxygen in the building. I have permanent lung damage because of the heat and smoke I inhaled in the accident. Some twenty operations later, doctors put me back together the best they could.

I am writing this true story to hopefully help someone else. The building I was trapped in was very small, approximately six feet by seven feet long and eight feet high, on the side of an asphalt tank with only one exit. After my accident, Ken Payne, who was in charge of safety, made all the pump houses with two exits.

Doing the type of work I did, I worked with my hands a lot. Things are much harder for me to do with only one hand. But I find a way that works. Things are getting easier for me with every day that passes. I am just very happy to still be able to do the things I enjoy doing. I am restoring my 1969 Pontiac GTO Judge, and I enjoy loading bullets, hunting, and renovating our home. So many people take things for granted in this world. This accident has changed my life in many different ways.

My first wife and I were divorced in 1997. I didn't think I would ever meet anybody ever again. I thought I would be alone for the rest of my life. My body has many scars, and I am missing body parts. But I met the person of my dreams, and we have lots of fun together.

I do things with a little more difficulty, but I get them done. I am enjoying my life with the different things challenging me, but I manage to get them done. By writing this true story, I hope to save someone else from going through the pain and suffering I have encountered with this accident and what it has put me through.

# Chapter 1

I was born to Sam and Evelyn Poletz in Biggar, Saskatchewan. I was from a big family of eleven siblings: Viola, Gloria, Laura, Kerry, Roger, David, Debbie, Marilyn, Connie, Brian, and Kevin. We lived on a farm six miles east of Landis, Saskatchewan.

My dad, Sam, farmed three-quarters of land. (He owned two quarters and rented one.) He was also a cattle farmer. We had about fifty or sixty head. We also had horses, pigs, turkeys, and chickens. We didn't have very much money.

My mom, Evelyn, grew three gardens so she had some vegetables for us kids to eat. We had a dirt basement in the house. Our potato bin was six feet wide by seven feet long and three feet deep. She would fill it full of potatoes for the winter. She would get big sacks of flour and make many loaves of bread a week so there would be some food in the house for her kids to eat.

My dad didn't care very much about what his kids had to eat. He was more interested in gambling most of the money away. In 1976, he sold the farm and moved to Biggar, where his gambling friends were. I continued my schooling in Biggar. I was now in grade eight. I got a job helping an old lady get her groceries, clean her walkways in the wintertime, etc. I also got a job at the ShopRite grocery store, where I eventually became the produce manager in charge of ordering produce and preparing it for sale. On October 8, 1979, I moved to Lloydminster, Saskatchewan, where I started work with Domtar Construction Materials on October 9, 1979.

*The plant where I worked for many years.*

The plant made a wide range of roof products, including three different kinds of shingles (True Seal, Low Pitch, and Permatite). It also made ninety-pound roofing felt. The plant had supervisors or a white hat for all the different areas in the plant—for example, production, lab, shipping, maintenance, and plant manager.

I started on the takeoff end, stacking shingles by hand and loading them where they came out into the warehouse. That was really hard work. Not many men would stay with that job. By this time, I had been at Domtar for two years

A few months later, a bid was posted for a forklift operator in the warehouse, a bid was posted I bid and got the bid. That was a very fun job. I quite enjoyed driving the forklift.

The manpower changeover at Domtar was huge at that point in time. Mr. Ken Payne was the production supervisor at the plant. He knew that loading shingles and stacking shingles by hand was a lot of physical labor. This is the main reason why he had a lot of respect for his men who stuck it out.

I had been with Domtar Construction Materials for nearly three years. I drove a forklift in the warehouse for about a year or so and did various jobs. My seniority was building so I could do whatever job I wanted. I moved around within the company for about six years, moving from job to job. I then drove a forklift in the north part of the plant's warehouse, where I unloaded limestone off rail cars into big tubs. The limestone was then dumped into a big bin that fed the machine. I didn't like that job very much. At the end of the day, you would be completely white from the limestone.

I eventually had enough of that job, so I moved again. Another bid was posted for the press section, I bid on the job and I got the job. I went back to production and ran the press. The press section was where the granules were pressed into the coating that was on the sheet. I ran the press for about a year. I didn't like that job too much either, it was also a lot of physical labor. The machine went from north to south. It was about a quarter-mile long. All the motors along the machine were a direct current motor. They could be started very slowly, and a thing called a rheostat could speed them up very quickly. The sheet traveled roughly at a speed of 250 to 300 feet per minute at full speed. With the direct current motor, you are able to vary the speed.

We had a room called the M.G. Room, which provided the power for the direct current motors throughout the plant. The machine started at the splicer's end, where big rolls of felt were brought in from the north warehouse and put on a big spool. You could put two rolls on the spool at one time. You could also move the rolls ahead on the spool. The sheet was threaded through the accumulator, a series of rolls that moved up and down. The accumulator would give you the time to make a splice. Once the new roll was spliced on, you were able to put the machine into one and one- half speed, which would bring the accumulator back down, which would bring the accumulator back down.

The asphalt we used in the saturator was a different type of asphalt. The asphalt was stored in two thousand-barrel tanks and heated to three hundred degrees. Then the asphalt was pumped into the saturator from the storage tanks. The sheet then went into the saturator through a series of "s" roles. The saturator had a big duct on top of it, which would suck the smoke and fumes from the asphalt into a room called the pollution room. The felt would then come out of the saturator, soaked with asphalt. It would then go through the drying section, where it would dry the sheet. Then it would go through the coating section, where the coating was put on the top and bottom of the sheet. The coating came from another thousand-barrel tank that was heated to 450 degrees Fahrenheit. A duct was on top of the coating pot, which would suck the asphalts, smoke, and fumes into the pollution room.

The pollution room was a big suction fan that sucked the fumes into a big chamber or piping system. The fumes then went through a series of filters before going back into the atmosphere. The sheet then traveled through the granule section, where granules were put on the sheet through a series of different shoots. The sheet would then pass through the press section, where the granules were pressed into the asphalt so they would now be fixed on the sheet in the form of a shingle, whatever kind we were making. The sheet was cooled with cold water spraying on it as the sheet passed through the press section.

Then the sheet went into the cooling looper loops. The cooling looper was about thirty to fifty yards long. The cooling looper was a series of bars spaced evenly apart so the sheet would make a loop and cool off. Big cooling fans were blowing air on the sheet. Also, cold water sprays were spraying cold water on the sheet as it passed by. The sheet was then pulled down to the takeoff end, where it was cut into three shingles as it passed through the cutter.

A machine called a winder was quite a conversation piece. The men would say they had thought it may have come over on Noah's Ark. The winder wound up the scrap felt and put it on the scrap pallet. We also used this machine when we made ninety-pound roofing or roofing felt. When we made ninety-pound roofing, we had a man operating the winder, someone wrapping the rolls of roofing, and two men loading the rolls on pallets. When we made roofing felt, two men were on the machine. One man would operate the winder, wrap the rolls, and roll it down a table when we had our coffee breaks. Two men from the warehouse would come in and relieve us for our coffee breaks, one man would operate the winder and one man would wrap and loaded the rolls of roofing felt on a pallet. I was the winder man for many night shifts.

Now I'll get back to shingles and the order in which they were made. The nip rolls were in front of the cutter. They would pull the sheet into the cutter, where it would be cut into three shingles. This machine was another conversation piece, the cutter came over on Noah's Ark with the winder. The cutting cylinder was a series of knives placed in a big steel roll in a certain order. The way they were placed in the cutting cylinder, they would cut three shingles in one revolution. This roll ran up against another steel roll with hardened rings in it where the knives ran. When the sheet went through the cutting cylinder, it would cut the sheet into three shingles at a very high speed.

From the cutter, the shingle would travel on the conveyor belts and then into a tray. There, they were put in bundles of twenty-one shingles per bundle by hand. Three people, one man on each tray, stacking shingles. They would then get pushed onto a conveyor, which took them over to the wrapper. They then would be packaged and marked. The shingles then went out on a long conveyor into the warehouse, where they were loaded onto pallets. They were stored in the warehouse racks for sale. The warehousemen would then load them on a big flatbed trailer, a closed-in trailer, or a boxcar and sent wherever they were sold.

I'll go back to my experience working at Domtar. Another bid was posted this time for granule man for the granule section, I bid and I got it. I then went to the granule section and did that job for six months. I didn't like that job much either. It was too precise for me. It was also very repetitive. I didn't like that. I was responsible for keeping the bins full and running the colors needed. I was a granule man for about six months. That job, like many jobs in the plant, I found very boring and repetitive.

Soon, I saw another bid posted for splicer, I bid and got it. 1 then went down to the north end of the machine and began splicing. I stayed doing that job for a few months. I didn't like that job much either. It was also very repetitive, and as you now know, I don't like that kind of work. Then another bid was posted, this time for cutter man. I bid on that job, and I got it. After a few months of running the cutter, I found I didn't like that job either because it meant being in charge of four men. Some didn't listen to orders, which made problems for me.

I kept looking for new bids. A bid was posted for the maintenance department. This time, it was the one I was waiting for. I had tried just about every job in the plant and didn't like any of them. This was the one I enjoyed immensely. It was always something different. The plant manager, Mr. Ken Payne, always found the time to visit me at whatever job I was doing, I started in the maintenance department, working under the supervision of Chris. I soon worked my way up, and I was doing everything the maintenance workers did.

I worked under Chris's supervision for quite a few years. Chris was small but mighty. Chris knew what he was doing in the maintenance department. He knew it like it was the back of his hand. We had a lot of fun and laughs. Chris was a lot of fun to work with. Chris was always a very happy-go-lucky person to work along with.

At this time, the maintenance supervisor was Gordon Ross, a very gruff old man. It was his way or no way. He was there for many years before he retired. We would call him the "computer" because he knew everything about the operation of the plant and where you could find things to fix problems that we encountered along with the machine.

Chris then became the maintenance supervisor in the 1990s. Once that happened, I started running my own shift. I had the experience I needed to take on this task. Chris becoming my boss was quite a blessing. I had worked with Chris for years. I thought this was something you would only dream about having happened. He had a lot of respect for me, and I had a lot of respect for him. Chris was paying me the wage of a third-year apprentice, which was very good of him.

I liked the maintenance department a lot because we were always doing something different every day. This was the kind of work I was destined to do, this was my job.

# Chapter 2

In the late 1980s, we did some major changes to the machines in the plant. The plant in Burnaby, BC, shut down. We got most of their machines, which were much newer then our machines were. The limestone system was changed, along with the granule section, these were two very big improvements to our machinery. Chris and I put a new cutter and automatic shingle stackers in place, these were two more very big improvements.

All these changes were very big improvements in our production. A room was built on the south end of the plant for the Permatite equipment. The machines were then put in that room to make the Permatite shingles. That was a very big improvement for the maintenance department. Because we no longer had a major product changeover, it cut down the hours for completion.

In 1991, an American company, Globe, purchased Domtar Construction Materials, and our name became Northern Globe Building Materials. We now had a longer yearly shutdown, which caused many problems along with the machine.

By this time, I was working in the maintenance department, the job I strived for, and enjoyed immensely. I was responsible for keeping the machines in top working order. We worked shifts from 7:00 a.m. to 3:00 p.m., 3:00 p.m. to 11:00 p.m., or 11:00 p.m. to 7:00 a.m.

I enjoyed the work I did, as it was always something different and involved repair work, which was always an interest to me. That is one thing about the millwright trade that I liked.

I was a third-year apprentice, and I was to go to school for my fourth year. My goal was to be a journey certified millwright. Under the new ownership, I noticed many changes at the plant. Some were very obvious; some were subtle. The management wanted more speed from the machines without spending the money to upgrade or repair the aging machines. Some of the more subtle changes were less focused on employees and work safety standards. Their main goal seemed to be to speed up production with little concern for quality loss or safety. As a result, I noticed we had more downtime than ever before with more work-related injuries.

I am now going to talk about another very bad thing that happened to me. On December 5, 1991, a friend and I went hunting deer in Art-Land pasture. That day was very cold, thirty-five degrees below zero. Art-Land pasture is roughly twenty-five kilometers southeast of Lone Rock. Art-Land pasture is about twenty-five miles square. It is a very big pasture. I was hunting with the same guy who was the quality control man at the time of my accident in 1992. It started to be a very cold but a nice, calm winter day. About 11:00 a.m., I shot a deer that was lying down at the time. I hit the deer because there was lots of blood. I began tracking the deer. Shortly after I started tracking the deer, it began to storm. The wind came up, and it started snowing very hard.

I couldn't even see my tracks behind me. It was snowing and blowing so hard. It was a good thing I was dressed very well. Tracking the deer in the storm, I soon got turned around and didn't know which way I was going. I never did find that deer. It ended up getting away. There was lots of snow that year. The snow was about three or four feet deep in places. I was having a very hard time walking through the deep snow. I had to get on my hands and knees and crawl over some of the snowbanks. I knew that, if I were to survive this, I would have to keep on moving. At times, that was very hard to do in the blizzard conditions

I was in. My body was getting very exhausted and cold. I had matches and a lighter on me because I was a smoker. I tried to light a fire, but I was unsuccessful in the blizzard conditions. I couldn't get a fire going. Even in a sheltered area, there was no small firewood or kindling, and I had no way of cutting what there was for wood.

I now had been lost in the pasture for about three or four hours. The pasture is very barren land, and it is a series of rolling hills with a few trees. Every hill looked the same as the last one I had gone over. The snowstorm was extremely bad. At times you couldn't see anything. I had shot a deer at very close range. I had to do something, or I would die.

It was the second deer I had shot that day. It was a matter of life or death. I was very cold. I cuddled up to the deer's body to try to get warm. I had a bullet belt on my waist, which held thirty rounds of ammunition, and it was full. I had now been lost in the pasture for five or six hours. It was now getting dark. I started firing shells into the air every few minutes, hoping someone would see the red streak go through the air. The people in Marsden, Saskatchewan, which is approximately five miles northeast of Art-Land pasture, set up a search crew on snow machines. The train tracks go right through the centre of the pasture. They also had the men on the train blow the whistle as they went backward and forward through the pasture. I heard the whistle and began going toward the tracks. It was now dark, but the sound of the train whistle really helped me.

They kept on blowing and blowing the whistle on the train. I kept on walking through the deep snow toward the train whistle. It was now about eight or nine o'clock at night. I had been lost for approximately nine or ten hours at this point. I was very frantic and scared that I wouldn't be found. I walked up over a hill and saw vehicle lights. I very quickly shot off my last three shells into the air. I then threw down my gun and waved my arms very aggressively. The lights on the vehicles picked me up against the white snow. The truck came up to me very fast. I was finally found. I got in the truck. The driver had turned on the heat full blast. That heat felt so very good. I was very cold. The driver was my friend, the same person who had come deer hunting with me that morning. I must have had an angel riding on my shoulders to get me through this ordeal.

My friend took me to the Marsden bar and got me warmed up a little bit. They had me wrapped up in warm blankets with heaters on me. They were also bringing me hot coffee to drink. Then I was taken to Lloydminster Hospital, where I was admitted and treated for hypothermia. They kept me in the hospital overnight to make sure I was doing fine. I had frostbite on the big toe on my right foot. Otherwise, I was doing very well. I was a very healthy, fit, young man.

The next day, I was released from the hospital. Then in March 1992, tragedy hit me again and very hard this time. So I went from being out in the deep-freeze to being put into the fire, or, in this case, 450-degree asphalt.

## Chapter 3

*The building where the terrible accident happened*

At approximately 4:50 p.m. on March 25, 1992, the quality control man came to me and said he was having trouble opening and closing a valve in the coating pot pump house. One of the quality control man's main responsibilities was taking the pump over of asphalt from the Husky Refinery that was right next to our plant. They supplied the asphalt that we stored in a thousand-barrel asphalt tank, and it was used in vast quantity to make shingles.

Maintenance workers would take the bung out of the valve, clean the grease grooves, and then put it back together and grease the valve. The quality control man informed me that the asphalt in the tank was lower than the valve we were working on so there wouldn't have been any problem.

With me using the above-described method of unceasing or freeing up the valve, I asked him if he was sure that it was safe to carry out this procedure. I double-checked with him before beginning to work on the valve. After my accident, my coworkers said the quality control man had just taken a pump over from the Husky Refinery. He should have known that taking apart the valve wasn't a safe thing to do. He didn't care; just make things easier for himself. The Husky Refinery would blow the line back with air so the line wouldn't be plugged for the next time it was used. The valve was an open-and-close flow valve, and it was in a closed position.

I started taking the valve apart. Two bolts held the bung in place. We heard a sudden rush of air, which would have been the air that Husky Refinery blows the line back with. Then two or three seconds later, out came boiling hot asphalt at a very rapid flow. The quality control man was in front of me, right in front of the doorway. He turned around and ran for help when he saw the heavy flow of hot asphalt escaping. Because I was on the other side of the valve, I jumped back. Otherwise, I would have gotten it right in the face, and the asphalt was 450 degrees Fahrenheit. I would have died if I would have tried to go through the heavy flow of hot asphalt. There was only one exit in the pump house.

The pump house was about six feet by seven feet long and about eight feet high. It was built on the side of the thousand-barrel asphalt tank. The building was made out of heavy sheet metal, two sheets of twelve-gauge metal about four inches apart with insulation between the sheet metal. This is considered a confined space and should have had more than one exit. I was now trapped, but this didn't stop me from trying to get out of the building. A massive spray of the boiling hot asphalt blocked the only exit. When asphalt goes into the open air, it causes a thick white smoke. I couldn't even see my hands in front of my face.

I was wearing coveralls, steel-toed work boots, and a hard hat. My hard hat fell off and melted from the heat. In the side pocket of my coveralls, I had various tools pliers, half-inch and nine-sixteenths wrenches, various screwdrivers, and a crescent wrench. These were some of the tools the maintenance department carried with them on shift. It was getting so hot that my toes started to burn from my steel toe in my work boots. I stood on top of some pipes, which were right where I was standing.

I thought, "There is a water sprinkler head in here, and if it goes off, I am dead."

When water hits the asphalt, that hot 450 degrees would cause the pump house to fill very rapidly as asphalt expands when it comes into contact with water when the temperature is that high. An exhaust fan was right above me. It was going, but that didn't stop me. I wanted out of that building. I thought I could maybe get through the hole in the wall where the exhaust fan was mounted to the wall. Three brackets were holding the exhaust fan on the wall. I got two bolts out, but the third was turning on the other side. The bolts went right through both sheets of metal. My tools were getting very hot quite quickly. I would drop it frantically and get another one, which seemed a little cooler. My hands were very badly burned at this point in time. I couldn't get the third nut off.

Adrenaline kicked in. I grabbed hold of one bracket of the running exhaust fan, pulling it off the wall and throwing it out the doorway. Then I tried to get out the hole in the wall. The hole was too small, and I couldn't get through. So I tried to tear the sheet metal to make the hole bigger. The metal was so hot that my hands were burning, but I didn't give up. There were pieces of skin on the wall where I tried to rip the hole bigger. My boss, Chris, was now on the other side of the building where the exhaust fan was on the wall. I put my left hand out through the hole in the wall. He grabbed it. He was holding me up from falling in the asphalt. It was getting to the point when the asphalt hit me that I couldn't even feel it anymore.

I could hear Chris yell to someone to get a cutting torch. He was frantic. Everyone who was around the building would have been killed if he would have gotten and lit a cutting torch. I thought I was going to die.

I said to Chris, "Tell my wife I love her."

The next thing I knew, my left foot slipped off the pipes I was standing on. Chris couldn't hold my weight any longer. About two seconds after that happened; I passed out from all the pain. While I was passed out, the men in the plant were piling shingle pallets up so they could get around and through the asphalt that was accumulating around the building.

The asphalt was now about six inches deep in places. The men tried everything they could think of to get me out. I had a lot of respect around that place. They would tell me, if you wanted something fixed right, call Dave. They first called the fire department. The fire department told them that this wasn't a matter for the fire department because it wasn't a fire. All this time, I lay passed out in the pump house.

They then called the rescue squad. When they arrived on the scene, it had now been approximately twenty minutes. There was now about a foot of asphalt in some places. Thankfully, the men had been piling up pallets so they were able to get around the building. Mr. Larry Gale, our plant electrician, was called to shut off the power to the building. He is a very big man but a very gentle one, and he has a heart of gold.

The maintenance men had already shut off most of the power to most of the building. This all happened after twenty minutes of being trapped. They then started cutting a hole where I was last known to be. The cutoff saw they were using was having a hard time getting through both sheets of metal at the same time. The cutoff saw was very heavy, and there were two layers to go through. They had to be very careful that they didn't touch me.

The rescue squad was just about through the two layers of metal. When they got through, they could see me lying there unconscious. They had to be really careful that no one else was hurt. That hot asphalt hits you and burns instantly and keeps burning until it gets cool. When they finally pulled me out, they all thought that I was dead. I had been trapped in the building thirty or thirty-five minutes in total.

*The clothing I was wearing at the time of the accident.*

They got me into the rescue squad truck. There was still a very faint pulse. On the way to the Lloydminster Hospital, my heart stopped three times. I was given mouth-to-mouth and revived. When I got to the Lloydminster Hospital, Mrs. Colleen Simona and Mrs. Pat Redden were the two nurses who started pouring normal saline on me to cool down my body temperature. My wife and family members were called to the hospital. The burns to my body were very deep and life-threatening. They thought a big percentage of my body was burnt. Some of the burns were so deep that they were affecting my breathing.

My wife and her doctor, Jill Lakins, got there. The doctor thought it looked very bad. My wife told her to do whatever it takes. She said, "I need him to live." The doctor then determined that, for me to live, I would have to be sent to University Hospital in Edmonton. They have a very fine burn unit there. They had to take me to the airport to have me transported from Lloydminster, Saskatchewan, to Edmonton, Alberta. Edmonton is approximately 248 kilometers… Lloydminster, Saskatchewan, is not a very big city. At the time, we didn't have a 9-1-1 service.

The rescue squad of Lloydminster, Saskatchewan, had the Lloydminster Royal Canadian Mounted Police block all major intersections on the way to the airport. I think Constable Ross Stevens also had something to do with that happening. He was a member of the Lloydminster Royal Canadian Mounted Police at the time of my accident and my neighbor for many years. At the time of my accident, we were good friends. I think he had all the streets blocked from the hospital to the Lloydminster airport.

I really would like to thank him immensely in person. He was transferred shortly after my accident. I believe they only stay in one place for seven years. Ross is now retired from the police force. I tried to get in touch with him quite a few years later, but I was unsuccessful in speaking to him.

I then arrived at the airport. A few minutes later, the Stars Air Ambulance got there. They weren't able to get the Stars Air Ambulance helicopter so they transported me by air ambulance jet to Edmonton Municipal Airport. It took them about twenty minutes to get to Edmonton, Alberta, from Lloydminster, Saskatchewan.

I was taken by ambulance to the burn unit in University Hospital. The course of my hospital stay was up and down because of my extreme burn injuries. The first time I was taken to the OR was five days after my accident. Three things that were the doctors' biggest concerns were my left leg, the fingers on my left hand, and the calf and Achilles tendon on my right leg.

# Chapter 4

Excerpts from the original document issued by the doctors in the burn unit at University Hospital in Edmonton, March 25, 1992.

Physical examination shows a young, fit-appearing male who was sedated and incubated. BP 150/80, heart rate 120, temperature 365.8. GCS 8/10. He is localized to pain, spontaneous eye-opening, and there was no verbal communication because he was incubated. Pupils were one min and pinpoint probably due to the sedation. He has a marked amount of kemosis in both eyes, left greater than right. Corneas were clear. Fundi were poorly seen.

Nose has an NG tube in. Mouth showed a slight oral swelling Chest exam showed good air entry bilaterally. Tube is in a good place on the chest x-ray CVS exam. Normal heart sounds with no murmurs. Right arm showed a good pulse to the left arm, pulse by Doppler only. Oximetry was able to pick up a pulse in the left fingers. Right leg, good pulses palpable. Left leg pulses well with Doppler only. Abdomen was soft and non-tender. MSK, no fractures or bruising. Skin, approximately 44 percent burn to both upper extremities and to lower extremities, areas of full-thickness, including left arm and left lower leg, and the right calf.

During resuscitation period, he required escherotomies of his left hand. Escherotomies were not done because there were pulses detected at all times. On March 27, a consult was put into pulmonary, and he underwent a fiber-optic bronchoscope, which showed mild erythematous. Change of mucosa with a small amount of whitish-yellowish secretions seen bilaterally.

Cultures taken from the sputum were sent and later returned as showing Klebsiella pneumonia and Hemophilus species. He was taken to the OR for the first time on March 30 by Dr. Moysa, where the burns were discovered to be a lot deeper than expected. In the right arm, there were full-thickness burns, but muscle was spared. Left arm, the fingertips were necrotic. Muscle was dead in many areas and had to be debrided. Right leg, there was dead muscle in the calf, which was resected partially. The Achilles tendon did not appear viable at the distal end, and the calcaneous was affected. In the left lower leg, all muscle compartments were necrotic.

Despite the palpable distal pulses, a consult intraoperatively was placed to orthopedics regarding a below knee amputation, which was performed during the same operation by Dr. Kortbeek. The patient required nine units of packed RBCs, Il L Crystalloid, and six units of saline during the first operation. On the second day postop, the patient developed a right pneumothorax and required placement of chest tube. Examination of left below knee stump on April 1 showed that the bulk of the muscle was healthy, but there was some superficial necrosis. The patient was kept ventilated postop and had various amounts of graft taken. He was taken back to the OR April 5 by orthopedics by Dr. Kortbeek because of developing muscle necrosis in the distal stump. He underwent excision of bone muscle and fascia over the left below knee stump. The flap was reapproximated throughout his stay.

The patient was kept on tube feeds and various antibiotics to cover the appropriate organisms. He was kept ventilated for most of his stay. He was followed by Infectious Disease Service. His second major burn operation was on April 8 by Dr. Moysa and underwent debridement, or scraping the dead skin. They then grew new skin for his left and right upper shoulders and posterior thigh. The patient was later growing

Methicillin-resistant Staphylococcus aureus after this operation, and he was placed on vancomycin. The patient improved after this, and on April 11, he was able to be extubated, which was done earlier in the morning, approximately eleven o'clock. The patient was well all day until evening when he developed respiratory distress and required reintubation.

After reintubation, the 02 saturation remained low. Chest x-ray was obtained, which showed a total collapse of his right lung. After aggressive chest physiotherapy with patient's left side down, he eventually began to mobilize some of the secretions, and the 02 saturation improved. The patient was taken back to OR for the third operation for his burns on April 16, 1992, by Dr. Lobay and under Dr. Kortbeek, where he underwent debridement and grafting of his left upper arm, left posterior thigh, and right lower leg.

He began growing Candida from many areas, and fluconazole was later added to cover this. Even since admission, the patient's mental status was poor. He gazed, occasionally head bobbed, and only occasionally obeyed commands elevating limbs. CT scan of the head was obtained, which was reported as showing diffuse widening of the suici over both hemispheres in the vermis. Consult was put into neurology, who felt that no further investigation need to be done at that time. Fourth burn surgery was done April 27 by Dr. Moysa, where the patient underwent debridement and grafting of multiple small areas with amputation of all digits on the left hand at the level of the proximal phalanx. Postop, the patient was able to be maintained without intubation or ventilation.

He did well for five days, and then one morning, the patient developed respiratory distress and required intubation. X-ray was obtained and showed a consolidated left lower lobe, and it was suspected that he had aspirated. The patient being fed at this time by tube feeds and by small amounts orally. It was shortly after this time several days later that the patient developed profuse septic shock with marked hypoxia and hypotension and required a large amount of fluids. He improved slightly overnight, and on May 6, he was taken to the OR by

Dr. Moysa, and a tracheotomy was performed. Patient was still quite sick at this time. He was placed on the appropriate antibiotics. Patient continued to improve from this point on, although slowly. On May 15, 1992, patient was taken back to OR by Dr. Tredget, where he underwent debridement and grafting of multiple small open wounds. He was also followed during this period by psychiatry by Dr. Collinson, who helped both him and his wife during this difficult time. The patient continued to improve and was able to be weaned off the ventilator. Patient's mental status also improved, although he was often still delirious.

During the next few weeks was basically a period of regaining strength and rehabilitation. The patient had two bone scans done during this period because of suspected heterotopic calcification because of decreased ROM in certain joints, including the right hand. Bone scan was not very helpful in that there were many areas of increased uptake. Consult was put in during this time to Glenrose Hospital for rehab there. He was eventually able to be transferred there June 15, 1992. At the time of discharge, the patient was up and about in a wheelchair. He had a left below knee amputation. All the digits on his left hand were necrotic. They were amputated. His left posterior thigh was removed. On the right leg, he is missing the calf and part of his Achilles tendon. He has 44 percent burns to his body.

He went from 195 pounds down to 133 pounds, so he is regaining his strength back. Tracheotomy site had closed over. He had several open wounds on the lower limbs, and he was still on multiple medications, including Senokot, Atarax, plain Tylenol, Tylenol #3, Didronel, Paramettes, Surmontil, Surfak, and Polysporin. He was to be followed up in burn clinic, and pressure garments had been arranged for the patient.

# Chapter 5

I don't remember too much of the time in the burn unit at University Hospital because I was put on a very high dose of morphine to keep me in a drug-induced coma from March 25 to May 15. Dr. E. Tredget, told me they had to do that. Otherwise, I would have died from the extreme pain from the burns and amputations. The burns are 44 percent of my body. I had my left leg amputated. All my left fingers were amputated. The right calf and left buttocks were removed. Work was also done on my right leg Achilles tendon.

I had to wear a full-body pressure suit or Jobst garments. They helped to keep the scarring at a minimum. I had two sets, a blue pair, and a green pair. That way, I could have my bath and have a clean pair to put on after my bath. They were like being tortured twenty-three hours a day. I had to wear the Jobst garments for three months after I was discharged from Glenrose Hospital. After the three months were up, I took them out to the Lloydminster landfill and burnt them. That is how much I liked those pressure suits.

After May 15 in the University Hospital burn unit, I remember a few things. When my wife, family, and friends came into my room, they had to be fully gowned with mask, hairnet, and gloves because of all the infections I was susceptible to getting. Because of the morphine, I was thinking about some pretty bizarre things. I thought my bathroom was a big truck that came every time the toilet flushed. Spiders were crawling all over the room. That morphine does very weird things to your body and mind.

When I first woke up, my room was right full of machines. There was a machine for my heartbeat, pulse, and blood pressure. A hose was coming out the side of my chest with a machine hooked to it. I was on a respirator breathing machine. A tube was down my nose with a machine hooked to it. My tracheotomy there was fitting on it' so they could disconnect and hook it up to the bagger. Now I could be transported to different areas in the hospital for tests and other things. They would put me in a big tub of quite warm water to debride my skin that was very painful. They would give me lots of pain medication before they did this procedure.

Physical therapy would come to my room in the early stage of my hospital stay. They would give me a shot of painkiller before they would start working on me. It hurt so bad that it brought tears to my eyes. I could hardly move my arms, legs, and hands in the beginning. Bone had started growing in all my joints from being immobilized so long. After quite a few weeks of rehabilitation in University Hospital, I began to hurt much less and less.

Then next thing I knew, I was being transferred to Glenrose Hospital, where I would undergo much more intense therapy from March 25 until I was transferred to Glenrose Hospital on June 15. My weight dropped drastically in that time. I went from 195 pounds to 133 pounds. They had me on a drink called Ensure, which was loaded with calories to help bring my weight back up to where I was before my accident.

At Glenrose Hospital, they worked on getting me moving, my arms, hands, and legs. They would have me up walking on my right leg to straighten my Achilles tendon and to help my balance. I would often go back to my room after the day, sitting there doing nothing. I would begin to hurt so badly that, even with painkillers, it would bring me to tears. I told the nurses about this. They got on this very quickly. They got me interacting with other people in the hospital. There was a game room where you could play lots of different games like cards, pool, shuffleboard, and other games.

After quite a few weeks in Glenrose Hospital, I was able to move my extremities much better. They started giving me a weekend pass. I could now go home for the weekend, but I had to be back on Monday morning. That was a very difficult procedure for me, but at the same time, it was great to get out of the hospital. The house that my first wife and I had in Lloydminster, Saskatchewan, was a front-to-back four-level split. The Workers Compensation Board (WCB) is an organization run through our government. They help injured workers who have been injured on the job or at the workplace. WCB and my wife did some alterations to our home so I was then able to come home.

They had chairlifts set up on the stairwells and wheelchairs on every level so 1 could move around in my own house. When I went back to Glenrose Hospital, physio had arranged to have me fitted with a prosthetic leg. Miss Leslie Arkesteiyn worked at Glenrose Hospital in the prosthetic department in September 1992. Leslie has a way of helping people that makes them feel very special. She is a very caring person and always does the best job possible. After I was discharged from Glenrose Hospital, Leslie remained to be my prosthetic girl. Shortly after I was discharged from the hospital, Leslie set up shop in Dewberry, just out of Lloydminster. I must say that made me feel very happy. I now would have a very competent prosthetic lady. Leslie made my first prosthetic leg back in September 1992. She does the Repairs on my prosthetic leg this very day. I like her work, and she does a very good job, even through all the problems I have had with my leg, like all the skin breakdowns I have had from lack of skin coverage.

Once I got my prosthetic leg, things seemed to start to get much easier. I now somewhat had some freedom back. I was able to get around and do a thing with much more ease. There are days I am not able to wear my leg, and I have to use my wheelchair, which makes things much harder.

The months went by pretty quickly. The next thing I knew, I was discharged from Glenrose Hospital. That was quite a blessing because I had been in the hospital for quite a long time. So from the day I got hurt, March 25, 1992, until September 25, 1992, I had been in University Hospital and Glenrose Hospital for six months all together.

When I got home, things in the house were all very well set up for me. My first wife and WCB had a girl come in to help me with things during the day, like taking medications, eating meals, and doing different tasks. She helped me for about two years. Then a very nice young lady replaced her. She and I had a lot of fun. She was a very fun person to have around. She would always make me laugh even if I was having a bad day, and I had lots of bad days. I needed someone like that after all I had been through. My first wife didn't have the time to spend with me. She was a photographer and owned her studio. She was a very busy lady. We were married on May 18, 1985, and we parted in 1997 after twelve years of marriage. This accident must have Impacted her more than it impacted me. I was no longer tall, dark, and good looking man. We were divorced due to what I now looked like. I would think that is pretty shallow.

After I was discharged from Glenrose Hospital, I had many operations to repair the problems I encountered. I had three major operations. I had many problems with my prosthetic leg fitting right because my left leg was burnt so badly. Dr. Tredget performed the first operation. He took the muscle from my left shoulder, which was slightly damaged from my accident, and put it on my left stump to give better coverage. So I would be able to wear my prosthetic leg more. That wasn't successful so Dr. Tredget then took the muscle from my right shoulder and put it on my stump. That was very successful. I could now wear my prosthetic for a few hours without getting a major breakdown. I was also having trouble with my heel on my right leg getting infected. I had infection after infection. It was so bad that you could see the bone. Dr. Tredget took the muscle from my right forearm and put it down on the heel of my right leg for better coverage. That was also very successful. The bone was now covered. There were no more infections from the bone being exposed. The only thing is that I now have a hairy heel. Through the years, Dr. Tredget has done many nerve-ending removals or neuroma surgeries, approximately every one or two years. This neuroma is very painful. I now have most of the problems I have had through the years fixed.

## Chapter 6

I then started getting out in the public more. Some people in society aren't very nice. For example, I was still in the University Hospital burn unit when this happened. They were giving me two-hour passes so I could leave the hospital for a break from things. My first wife and I went to West Edmonton Shopping Mall. I was in my wheelchair that day. We went by a young man who was selling puppets in the mall. He was talking for the puppet.

He said to me, "I would give you one of my legs, but they don't work very well either."

That was a very rude thing to say. That put me in tears. My first-wife went to the manager, telling him what the young man said. The manager fired him on the spot.

I would try to make sure my body was covered very well after that day. I would even go through the trouble of hiding my left hand. It must be human nature to stare at something different. This is one of the biggest reasons for me writing this book. I hope people will understand my situation better.

Some people in society now treat me like I am an outcast or like I am totally brain dead. Some people will stare at me, making me feel like I am a bug. Some people are quite compassionate and ask what happened to you. That isn't a very nice way to be treated after all I have been through. I am missing body parts and my speech is different because of my tracheotomy. I was in a bad accident that hurt me more physically than anything else. It is a free world, and people can think whatever they want. I don't really care because I have lots of people who know what I went through. They are all very understanding and are my best friends. My wife Lisa loves me, and I love her. She is my very best friend, and that is one thing that really matters in this world. From the way some people treated me, I thought I would be alone for the rest of my life, but Lisa changed that. We now have each other, and the way Lisa treats me, she inspires me to keep ongoing.

Before my accident, I was a very avid hunter. I had purchased a Sako 7mm Magnum just for big game hunting. A few days later, I was in my accident at work. I never did get the chance to fire that gun before my workplace accident. In 1994, I was able to fire that gun. I also went hunting that fall.

I got back into loading my own bullets as I did before my accident. For years, my brother-in-law, Neville-Johnson, has loaded his own bullets. He helped me get back into that and many other things. I also went hunting in the fall of 1995. That felt so very good to be able to do that again. I went north of the North Saskatchewan River, approximately fifty kilometers north of Lloydminster. When I got there in the morning about 6-am, I traveled the back roads. I came across a buck and a doe together. They were about 450 yards away from me. I couldn't see them very well with a naked eye. I put the gun out the window of the truck and took my time. I have a permit that allows me to legally shoot from my vehicle.

I had a very good rest and knew my gun's trajectory. I used a 120-grain ballistic tip bullet that travels at thirty-four hundred feet per second when it leaves the muzzle. At 450 yards, it will drop approximately twenty inches. I aimed just over the back of the deer and compensated for the drop. There was no wind that day. I hit him right where I was aiming. That 7mm and my hand loads work very well together. I then went over to the deer and tagged him. Then I went to a nearby feedlot. The guy at the feedlot helped me load the deer into the back of the truck. I took the deer to Lloyd Packers in Lloydminster, Saskatchewan, where they dressed the deer. When he was gutting the deer out, he said to me that this deer only had half a heart. I had made an excellent shot on the deer being the distance he was away from me.

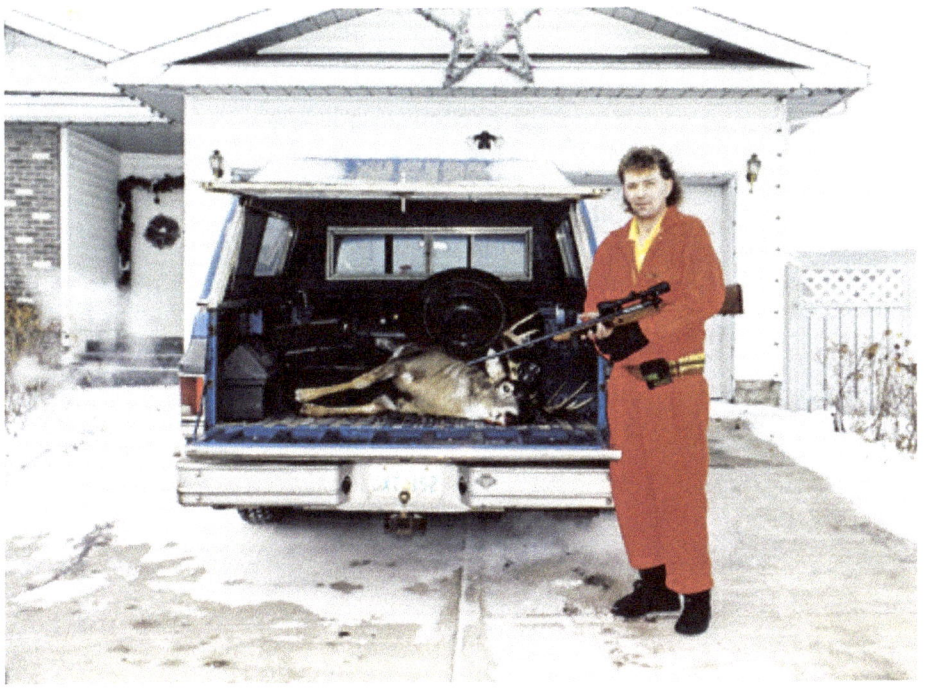

*My first deer after my accident*

I enjoy coyote hunting as well. It is a lot of fun when you have the right tools to do a good job. In the early 1980s, I bought a Sako Tikka 22-250. I shoot probably two thousand to three thousand rounds through the gun. The barrel was worn out. The accuracy was totally gone. My brother-in-law, Mr. Neville Johnson, and I were talking on the phone.

He said to me, "You need the proper tool to do the job. Bullet placement on a coyote makes a big difference if you get him or he gets away."

Neville found me a gunsmith in Biggar, Saskatchewan, which is where my mom lives. So the gunsmith, Mr. Bob Murch, put a new stainless steel barrel on my gun. Ted Gaillard Precision Rifle Barrels made the barrel. They are very fine barrels and have won eleven benchrest championships throughout the world. The gunsmith did some other work. He also glass floated the barrel. Trued and Blueprinted the action and also lapped the bolt lugs. Bob set the trigger pull down to one pound and six ounces. The gunsmith also put a muzzle brake on the gun, which helps on long-range shots.

The coyote doesn't know where the bullet comes from, as long as you are not moving around. I then purchased a 3.5 to 10 Leupold scope for the gun. Neville has a target dot in the scope on his gun he uses for hunting coyotes. Neville has been into loading bullets for years and many other things to do with guns, I took his advice. Before I put the scope on the gun, I sent the scope to Oakatoks, Alberta, and had a target dot put in the scope. Now I was ready to shoot at the coyotes and get them. At 100 yards at the range, I have put more than one bullet in the same hole. Every time I have gone to the range, and more then one time I have put a bullet in the same hole. These bullets are my hand loads, and I have done a lot of different preparations for my brass and other things. I am using a 40-grain V-Max moly coated ballistic tipped bullet. These bullets work great, and all these little things I do are all thanks to Neville and his loading experience, which he has shared with me through the years.

I live in Saskatchewan so I can use an electronic call to hunt coyote. The coyote will come running in very cautiously like his dinner bell is ringing. The coyote has three senses, and he uses them all very well to survive. A coyote hunts for food at night. (He is a nocturnal animal.) When I or anybody else goes hunting, the coyote is now the hunted, so they have their three senses very well or to the max for survival.

Their number one sense is their sight so you can't be moving around, or they will spot you right away. The coyote will not come into the call. I hunt coyotes from the middle of November until the end of March. At this time of year, it is normally very cold, and hard to not move at all from the extreme cold. This time of year is when the furs are their best for the fur buyer. I sell the coyote pelts to a fur buyer to cover some of the cost.

Back to the coyote, they have an advantage because you don't know which way they are going to come into the call. If they come in the wrong way and you move, they are gone right now.

Number two, their hearing is ten times a human's. So they can hear very well. They can hear a mouse squeak under the snow more than 100 yards away.

Their third sense is their sense of smell. If the wind is the wrong way or too strong, you might as well stay home. Neville has taught me all these things about coyote hunting, and he has killed hundreds of coyotes. I think coyote hunting is the best fun a man can have with his clothes on. It is a very competitive sport.

My health doesn't let me get out as much as I would like. I managed to get out a few times with my neighbor, Laurent Lavouie, during the winter. Lisa has also come coyote hunting with me quite a few times. She knows how I really enjoy the sport. In the past years, many different people have come hunting coyotes with me. I did get twenty-seven coyotes last winter so I tricked a few. All the work the gunsmith did on my gun has paid off. The fact that good optics were put on the Sako Tikka 22-250 that I use for coyote hunting, a coyote standing at three hundred to four hundred yards is in big trouble. Because if you know how your gun shoots and you have a good rest, he will probably be going for a ride in the back of your truck.

## Chapter 7

I've stayed in touch with a lot of the people I worked with at Northern Globe for many years. Then in 1997, a former coworker introduced me to his mother-in-law on December 5, 1998. I met the little lady who turned my life around in many ways. Lisa is the best thing that has happened in my life. She treats me like I am still a person, and she is my very best friend in this world. Lisa gave me a reason to live, and everyone needs that. I don't know that I would still be here if I didn't meet her. I don't go to church, but in this case, I have to say, "Thank God!"

My sister, Mrs. Gloria Johnson, had arranged this fly-fishing trip for her husband, Neville, my brother Roger, and me. Lisa presented it to me on my birthday in May 2001. Lisa is such a very wonderful lady.

On June 16, 2001, Neville, Roger, and I went on this fly-fishing trip to Brownell Lake. I had purchased a new Chevrolet Silverado in 1999. We took this vehicle on our trip. We drove to Deschambault Lake, 180 miles north of Prince Albert, Saskatchewan, a seven- or an eight-hour drive from Lloydminster, Saskatchewan. On the night of June 16, we stayed overnight at the Northern Lights Lodge.

When we got up in the morning, we were standing

Out in the yard. Neville, Roger, and I were talking to Mr. Ted Olson, the man who owned the Northern Lights Lodge and the fly-fishing camp. He was in a hunting accident where he lost sight in both his eyes. We were out in the yard talking. He was moving around in the area where we were talking when he ended up walking into his horse and He stumbling. This man is amazing.

He said, "That must have been my horse."

The horse was made from old tires. It is incredible how the other senses take over for the ones you have lost.

Time flew by very quickly. The next thing, we knew it was 8:30 a.m., time to pack up the plane and fly out to Brownell Lake. We were only allowed to have seventy-five pounds each. This included fishing gear, sleeping bag, food, beer, and whiskey. The pilot was very lenient about the weight we were allowed to have. The plane was a four-seater, single-engine Beaver with pontoons on it so it could land on water. The Beaver is a very well used bush plane.

We started on our flight to Brownell Lake, which was about one hour away. We would be up in the air may be two thousand feet. Then all of a sudden, we would hit an air pocket, and we would drop a few hundred feet. When this happened, it was a pretty scary ride. But I loved it! I would do it again in a heartbeat. It didn't seem very long, and we were landing on Brownell Lake.

We got all our stuff off the plane. We would be there for four days. We were all very excited to check the campout. We had many things there like: boat motors, gas, and a big block of ice in an ice house with a pick to take what we needed for ice. There were the men's and ladies' outdoor bathrooms and three cabins with a propane stove for cooking. With an outside fire pit for cooking, we had everything we needed. We then put our things away in one of the cabins. This would be our home for four days. That day, we all could not wait to get out fishing. It was great! That was the best time I ever had in my life! You would cast into the water, and 90 percent of the time, you would catch a fish ... and a big fish! We ended up not fishing for the whole day. Because we didn't need to. Just about every time you cast out, we would get a fish. Four days went by way too quickly!

Next thing we knew, we were waiting for the plane to come and get us to go back to Deschambault Lake and our vehicle. We had brought a cooler full of fish home for the wives to enjoy. We talked about this fishing trip and how it was the best experience in our lives. I really enjoyed that fishing trip, and I would do it again in a heartbeat.

The trip home seemed very long, but I was very excited to see my new fiancé

Just a few days after, we were married on July 7, 2001. We are now married and are a very happy couple. Lisa and I have done many things together. I have never had so much fun with someone in my life before. We go camping and take drives in the country together. We went to Yellowknife in the Northwest Territories. We went to British Columbia to visit my brother and his wife. We have done renovations on our house together. She is a very special lady. She helps me with everything. We lived in our house in Lloydminster until I sold it in 2000.

Lisa has a house in Lone Rock, Saskatchewan, twenty-nine kilometers from Lloydminster. My brother, Roger, has helped me with lots of renovations to our home. He is into woodwork and enjoys it immensely. We settled in Lone Rock, where we did major renovations to our house. My brothers-in-law on my wife's side, also friends, helped me pour the cement pad for the thirty by the forty-foot garage. My brother Roger and many friends helped us construct the garage. Then I removed the porch that was on the back of the house. I had the hole dug for the basement addition. My wife and I built the forms for the footings and poured them. Then we formed the basement walls, poured them, and built the floor. My brothers, Roger and Brian, and I built a much bigger addition, sixteen feet by twenty-two feet on the back of the house. Roger then helped me build a huge deck on the back surrounding the addition. Through the years, my wife and I have completed many renovations to our house.

I am now going to take you back to October 1979 when I started with Domtar Construction Materials. I purchased a 1969 Pontiac GTO Judge from the guy who was holding my hand back when I was trapped in the pump house. That guy's name was Chris Christiansen, my boss at the time of my accident. I drove this vehicle for six years or so. It was a very fun car with lots of power.

Then in May 1985, I was married to my first wife. The car was then parked and covered and sitting on a pad in my backyard. I kept that car, hoping that someday I would rebuild it. In 2005, I started that project of rebuilding that car, and I enjoyed every minute of it. I went all the way, pulling the motor and rebuilding it. I had the block bored out 040 and had the heads rebuilt by Meridian Engine Service Ltd. in Lloydminster, Saskatchewan. I purchased eight new pistons, a new camshaft, a new oil pump, new valve lifters, new rings, and a gasket set. I then started putting the motor together.

When it came time to put the pistons in the cylinders or in the block, being that I only have one hand now after my accident. My mom, Evelyn Poletz, who is now seventy-five years old, helped me put the pistons in the cylinders. Mom was down visiting with Lisa and me at the time. After I finished assembling the motor on a motor stand, I secured a chain block from the garage ceiling to the motor so it wouldn't move. I put ear protection in and then started up the motor for a few seconds. It ran well, filling my garage with smoke instantly. The motor was now ready to be put on the frame.

I have a hoist in my garage, which helped immensely. I then pulled the body off the frame and had the frame and body sandblasted at Christie Corrosion in Lloydminster, Alberta. I then primed and painted the frame. Then I started putting the frame back together. I then put the motor back on the frame. After the body was cleaned up, I then undercoated it inside and the underside. I then put the body on the frame and started repair on the body. I changed both the left and right quarter panels with new ones, along with both new left and right fender wells. Then I got a new left and right door skins. My wife and I then changed both door skins. I then got new left and right fenders, along with a new hood, and put them on the car. Then I had the dash recovered, and I installed it. I have had the motor running, and now instead of pushing the car around, I can drive the car. It runs very well. The car is now starting to look like a car again. I have put many hours into the restoration of the car. It will not be long before it will be going to the body shop to be painted the factory color. I will then be putting many more new parts on the car. In another year or so, I hope it will be done, and I can't wait for that day.

I finally finished my car approximately six years from the day I started. It had a four-speed Muncie transmission in the car. I then changed the transmission to a five-speed Kessler T.K.O-600 transmission. I did a few little upgrades to the motor and power train. It has headers, 670 Holley dual pump, M.S.D. electronic ignition, and electronic fuel pump. I also put a role cam in it with roller lifters and rockers. All these things make it a pretty sweet car to drive. I recently installed a set of latter bars on the back differential.

*1969 Pontiac, GTO Judge*
*My Flowerpot*

I am now going to take you back to the pump house where I was trapped. In March 1992, Mr. Ken Payne, the head of safety at the plant, had two exits put in all pump houses in the plant right after my accident happened. He also designed a wall that would drop over if the pressure was put on the wall.

Ken was also everybody's second dad in the plant. He especially took a liking to me. After my accident, the maintenance protocol changed drastically. We all knew each other very well at the plant, especially the men who were there for many years. The maintenance department now had to have a work order for any repairs done on the machine. That meant no more favors for anybody in the plant, even though we knew each other very well. Ken has now passed on. God bless his soul.

I am so happy I am still able to do things. My wife and I are a very happy couple. We have lots of fun together. My wife is my very best friend, we love each other, and that is all that matters in this world. I am in lots of pain, but life goes on. I just ignore it and go do something. I keep thinking to myself that if I had done something differently, this accident wouldn't have happened. I know that if there had been a second door in the building at the time, I would have walked out the door and not have been hurt at all.

It has now been just about twenty years since my accident. And I feel the pain and relive it every day that goes by. I now do a thing differently, but it is a big satisfaction to get something done. I now do things differently by maybe using a clamp or making a tool to get the job done.

The safety standards have changed majorly since the year my accident happened in 1992. There were lots of workplace accidents all over the globe. The government stepped in. Now the employer and employee can be held responsible. The employer and employee can both be fined or serve jail time if codes are not followed. Lockout procedures must be followed when working on any machinery. A confined space must have a minimum of two exits. The pump house I was in when my accident happened would be a confined space. That wouldn't be allowed.

# Burned Alive

As you have read, I have my wife, my car, and my guns, and I try to have a positive attitude about everything. I also have many other good things happening in my life. I have been on quite the journey through life. I still enjoy my life and the things I am still able to accomplish.

www.ingramcontent.com/pod-product-compliance
Lightning Source LLC
Chambersburg PA
CBHW041309240426
43661CB00045B/1499/J